I0822185

Dysphoria

DYSPHORIA

SHANE NEILSON

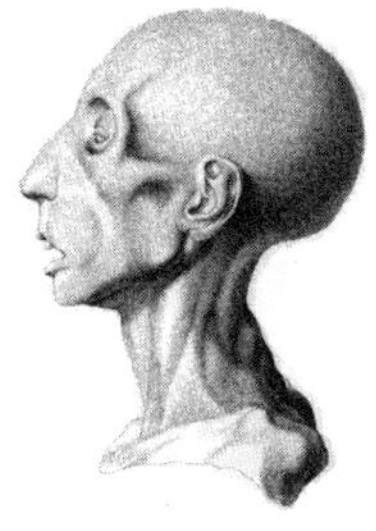

The Porcupine's Quill

Library and Archives Canada Cataloguing in Publication

Neilson, Shane, 1975–, author
Dysphoria / Shane Neilson. — 1st edition.

Poems.

ISBN 978-0-88984-402-5 (softcover)

I. Title.

PS8577.E33735D97 2017 C811'.6 C2017-900438-7

1 2 3 • 19 18 17

Published by The Porcupine's Quill, 68 Main Street, PO Box 160, Erin, Ontario NOB 1TO. http://porcupinesquill.ca

Readied for the press by Jim Johnstone.

Represented in Canada by Canadian Manda.
Trade orders are available from University of Toronto Press.

We acknowledge the support of the Ontario Arts Council and the Canada Council for the Arts for our publishing program. The financial support of the Government of Canada through the Canada Book Fund is also gratefully acknowledged.

For the feeling that feeds

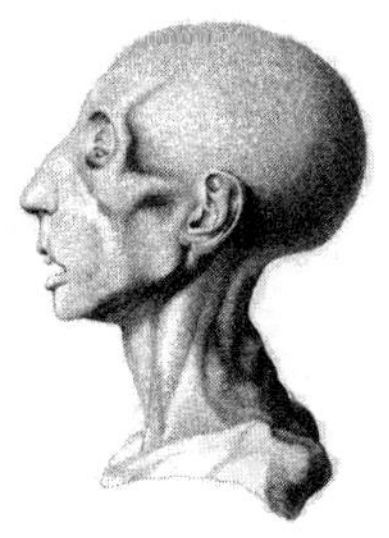

Table of Contents

PART ONE

The Grand High Medium Abominable

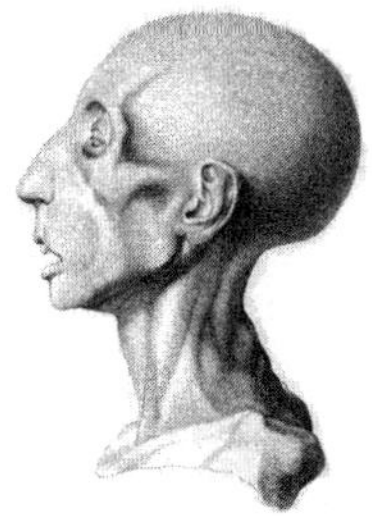

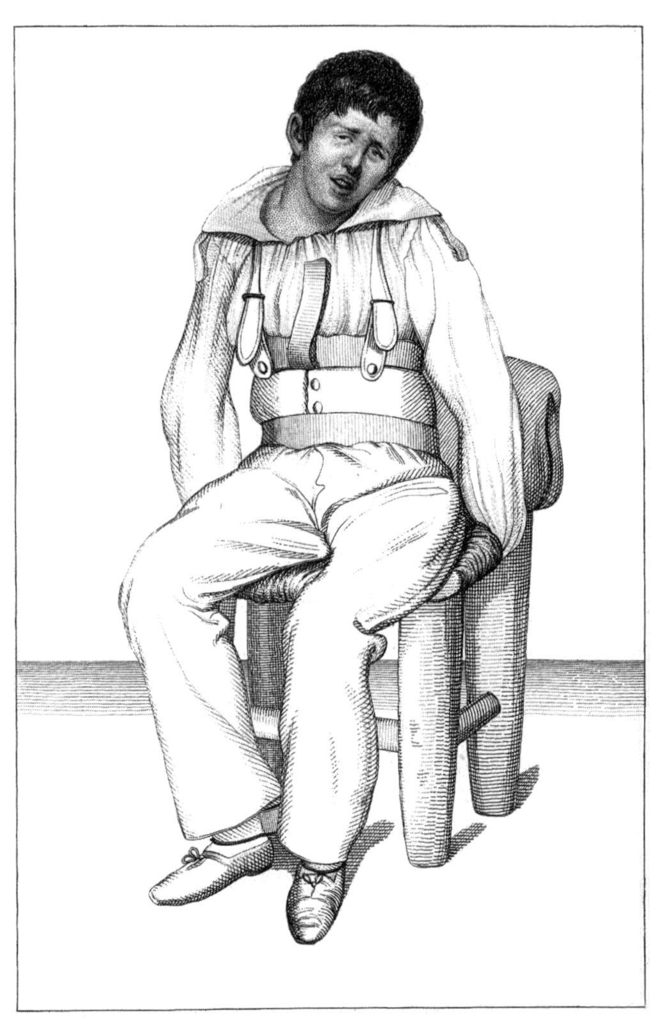

Dysphoria

Pain in this sense is more an occasion for art than a cause
—David Morris

I.

Emotion distilled into ampoules, the inoculate
roaring at the head of the needle—who needs

depot when the body's flooded with feeble?
Perhaps the lobotomy was the right thing to do,

back when you said you understood me and, ha,
no—I understood you. In the car park, at Big Park,

Little Park, in grocery aisles, in community rinks;
past security checkpoints and through turnstiles,

it was all darkness. To the coasts, I roar:
When a man loves a woman, he can't keep his mind.

Oh needle of lonesome, here's my ass one more time.
Last night, you asked, 'How does it feel?'

Percy? Sing for us? *She can bring him such misery*
if she plays him for a fool. This anthem serves the lost

in lieu of help; that's how it feels, old and good
bodies. Raise your right index finger and say

goodbye to the fool that points between your
eyes. The sensor never lies. It identifies.

2.

In the visible, we caper. Only the wall has our backs.
In the dock, our souls are in hock and we contest

the null exchange: love fell from the wall and couldn't
be put back together again. You know pain, it demands

compensation in America, while in Canada, the needles
are free. The same poisonous need is in our grammar

and that need is *we*. Hunger, desire, synonyms
for ruin, alternate sources to fuel arson, star-charts

for constellations we don't know are already gone:
billions of beautiful, snuffed stars we still see.

Cheshire is the smile that hides the friendly lies.
Off with your head and grind up the pill, smile cocktail-

face because everyone else will. Get saved before
Revelation. Spoiler: paranoid grace looks like {{}}

on the face. Though sensors identify, all I see is suffering,
a thousand names for pain refreshing like screensavers

and placed like wafers on tongues. Hey—your ass
remembers why you're here. Nietzsche sends his needlepoint

regards. Muscle memory is acquired from practising screams.
Not grimaces, but dream of when we were young, reading

tabulae rasae of the palimpsest, keys to futures and futures
of throw away the key. *Hey hey, my my,* stick a needle

in your eye, are you an adolescent with the can't-ever-die
fantasy? Did you just walk away? Are you a believer on

the other end of the line?

3.

Puritanicals burn at the stake while witches watch.
In Hades's soft middle the middle class yearns. Sky

riots to azure. Pure from purging cures, we can't lose
what we know. Go back to Genesis—we ate the fruit

from the tree. Didn't we? The lost are found. New losses
levy fees. Who among us *allows* us; who are we? Nemeses

are our loves, for the plural *us* went bust. We rust in the self's
Catherine Wheel. Feel self scrape the dome. Roam down

random roads to wander toward Rome. Home will be the last
place we find, the first place we lose. Nemeses coalesce

into a singleton. Your suburb screams. Balance like the sun
on the floor. Take more time to decide until the right decision

is time. Whispered by your nemesis as he passes in the hall:
This too shall pass. Build more channels for the oncoming song.

Lack isn't the catastrophe, nor excess. It's express, the disharmonic
that became the tinnitus you ignored. *Ding dong*, the witches sing.

Ding dong, ding dong. Drug-Day raged; night rose. Now, equipoise;
hubris leaks out the syringe's top.

4.

Climb the water tower Climb the water tower Climb the water tower Climb the water tower Climb the water tower Climb the water tower Climb the water tower Climb the water tower Climb the water tower Climb the water tower Climb the water tower Climb the water tower Climb

The reasons to live are not dependent on reason.
The reasons to live are not rational.

We all have a refrain, an earworm power-chording through the brain.
Once, it was *I love you*—
I sang to all the faces in love.
O, life jacket, I forgot to put you on. Now

Climb the water tower Climb the water tower Climb the water tower Climb the water tower Climb the water tower Climb the water tower Climb the water tower Climb the water tower Climb the water tower Climb the water tower Climb the water tower Climb the water tower Climb

5.

When push comes to shove, the asylum incarcerates.
Wrist-blades, neck-tourniquets, and plate glass ask

the DSM why. O otherkin, have you yearned to be quiet
and happy in bed? Were you led here, or congregate of your

own accord? Have you yet spoken to the dead? Have you
seen strange lights after bar fights, inhaled paranoid air

that was put there before you knew? Have you gnashed
your teeth? Weeped at the end of the world? Been seized

by serge suits in cruisers? What's worse: losing our minds
or losing ourselves? Not the same thing, self as static-cling.

I'm in love with you, the trueline, in love—
follow it back, you'll find the dashboard recording.

6.

Smartphones sprout legs and march while wives
and husbands rename the Panic Room to Pleasure Zone,

pressing Record. I, too, fell in love with the lie and the lie
saved me, it whispered *cost benefit analysis*. I sold my soul

to liberty, life, and pharmacology. Easy-peasy lemonade
squeezay, in the stadiums—salvation? In the stadiums.

In the stadiums, hear the hum of smartphones policing
the seas, maple syrup sticking to our earphones. Charon

wears a branded Hoodie. I've got Sketchers on and this here's
crotchet rock. I'm suburbo-dad. I thought it would all

work out, you know? But hard work isn't strategic. Work
smarter, but don't fear the first responders? The smartphone

in my tinfoil hat says that I've misunderstood. In the stadiums,
I lose the signal of another death-by-cop. *Ze plane, Ze plane*

says Tattoo on *Fantasy Island*. Upgrade: *Ze drone, Ze drone.*
The pictograms from the Lascaux tickertape *F-E-A-R-I-T-S-E-L-F.*

Faith is hard. Sammy Yatim needed the depot shot but the cop's
gun gave him lead poisoning instead. *Off with their head*

said the first responder. His gun said, *blam blam blam*
(pause)   *blam blam blam blam blam blam.*

Not first responder, final responder. As *Climb the water tower*
thrums through this dull skull, I take my mental temperature

about the police. *Just say Shane went crazy.*
That's why we shot him. He was a danger to others. (No, a

danger to myself.) Another refrain: *Who has performed*
and accomplished it, calling forth the generations

from the beginning? So the last shall be first,
and the first last. Sensor, protect me better

than you protected Sammy or I'll put you on loop,
broadcasting a still of Sammy unable to get up,

(pause) unable to get up (pause) unable to get up,
(pause) unable to get up (pause) unable to get up,

(pause)—
that's sunlight balancing on the floor

7.

So long as the paperwork's clean, you boys can do
what you like out there. The National Fear's too dear,

grand statements of our love left cyanide mines across
the Canadian Shield. And we shall not yield, my fellow

Canadians! We already kneel in beheading videos. Hold me
closer Tiny Dancer, to the Pleasure Zone wickedness comes.

In the stadiums, in the stadiums, Love the Virus goes Zika.
For protection, I finger the selfie screen. Who is the saviour

of us all? I nominate you to slip by undetected past lives,
beyond sensors of areas public and private. Of censor

and insensate. I'm dying. But no shit—by the power
of love do I so invest thee, and that I am so invested. Sensor,

dost thou witness secrets or encrypt their data? Chorus, chorus,
chorus. Stanza, stanza, stanza. No—wrong image of loss.

The image bank's a blood bank run by the Red Cross.
My question's fuse lit, I change. Voiceless, we shall

give thanks to the sensor. Then we shall be restful,
fuck the affidavit! But the song says no, and Percy

sings no: *Loving eyes can't ever see.* Revenant in desire,
policies are for police to lock up the free. Dunk my head

in the Styx, suspend me from one wrist, tell me I'm Achilles
until Paris arrives with absinthe and an arrow, all delirium

is expansive, we lie down when we're mute in asylums
for the wrong, no myth or no man or no mind. This advice

to escape the serge suits and anyone who hurts: never take
the white frightful drugs. But that's not why we fall in love

in the first place, just to hang on to life. Right?
Wrong song. *Climb the water tower.*

8.

Uniformed perpetrators flee. Their getaway car hits
a little girl on the careen. People point, priests anoint,

and the day goes on, covered under the sun. Dysphoric,
in the grand high medium abominable, I put the cover story

in Park at its end-time. Past the rink, pool, and church,
I now wonder at the pier. Percy's outta here.

Rita Charon advocates Radical Doubt. *Be Radical
Doubters!* Oh Rita, we're too naïve. At further

redoubt, the fist or caress is the same mess. Such
is my conclusion, not a proof. The crate or pedal,

the gold metal on flesh, the goodbye, the why,
the depot timing and the depot timed, concentrate

on the far point as part of you, ___________ over,
and in the sensor's swath there will be beauty beyond

the sour red smear. Flood the threshold and say,
This is all you can do to me, all you've ever done.

Dysphoria saturates oblivion. How now? How now.
The suburb sky is burnt by enforcement, the pier's

horizon reddens with National Fear. Sailor's warning:
I want another, hand clasped, heavy and sleeping,

in the dark—

9.

Because you need a puncture to bleed sorrow-ward,
toward the shot of no point, move backward from your

finger to the wrist where a clock lingers, reverses,
is severed by Salvador D. Farther up, you lick face

tattoos. Drop down to an abdomen not topsy-turvy,
but inny-outy. Emotion's not inoculate but involution,

a high-volume embrasure that radiates the common bond.
The index finger points to lowdown. We're a gutter us,

but the world's in opposite sheen: glare from a blinking
sensor that overrides despair. *Blink.* The world giveth

and the world taketh away. Cops come with roo-roos
but the siren is self. They lash your old and good body

to a mast that lets your worst be worse. How were you
tied? Wiggle your finger, Axis I Houdini, escape to the

Quartermaster chapter. Quaker Ahab and Ishmael agree:
we all drown. *From hell's heart they stab at thee!*

A destructive element creates the goodness that happens
away from us. Oh, it's all in your head. And all in your

head is why you sing, and you sing for them. A star
connects with an eye. Percy, your two cents please:

Sleep out in the rain. There, pain escapes sensor detection
and lives in the old, good brain. Finger, this direction, over

here: this is the church, this is the steeple, this is how you
interact with delusional people. How now? How now.

In love, you conduct, *I am so very much in love.*
I owe all my success to brimstone from above.

10.

My people are easy to mock and to lobotomize but hard
to fix. No warranties or guarantees for the old and good

body except: beauty is what happens when Murphy's law
applies. Sensor, don't testify. That's what *we* do. You identify

life, mark the flatfoots in lockstep with lovers who fall out
of line, AWOL with Reverend Jim Jones. His testimony on love

as weapon: *I've got a hell of a lot of weapons to fight!*
I've got my claws. I've got cutlasses. I've got guns.

I've got dynamite. You know the fallacy of proving we're
in this together when selfishness is what we *do.*

The palliative for pain is not end, cure, or netherworld
of drug. Not love. Not sky-chaplains, Mommies or ghosts

in machines, but refusing more.

II.

What is visible to LED eyes and rented surveillance
systems that detect burglars, but not thefts in the night?

Reverend Jones's finger ➤ dysphoria throws acid from half-glasses
but drinks some first to be fair. Tip a glass on the house,

ripple the surface of water, of moons. The Yield sign
poses more challenge than Stop. Shall not, shall not,

if you go to sleep before you rest, stabilizers won't bind

to your receptors. Express the catalogued genome as rave,
rant: the world's not crazy, it's claustro. Distinguish words

in pain and discover the difference between authority and
intuition. We all choose to hear, or not to choose to hear.

Loosed to speak of horror: sad prophet clowns and their kin
with the common moan from the embrasure, *I too*

have a certain kind of hurt, I too bear wounds you can dive
into and be loosed—all is null in this hell of unrest,

though you've heard that you are blessed. In Times
Square, a man on a crate advises, *Raise your voice*

in song. Michael, Row the Boat Ashore, Hallelujah.
How many blinks before we're gone? Blink once,

twice, or evert eyelids. Press Record. The sense is fine,
and high, and my dear, you look beautiful tonight.

12.

Self as static-cling, as ain't no thing, as bored debriefing?
Sure. *Strategies to overcome.* In business chic, monarch gloom,

Reverend Jones intones: *Off with their stuck, off with their stuck,*
off with their stuck. Doubting Thomas says, *Why the fuck?*

In the body is evolution. We long, so cells make lovers' leap.
Friends advise, *Keep well.* In revivalist tents in the American

desert, Jim Jones clones shout, *See you in hell.* Poems
stall like cars. Traffic encases in amber. Embers are Day-Glo.

In the hypnagogic horizon that's birdsong-free, recognize dimly:
longing elegizes what's wrong. We erect monuments to strange

pasts that aren't what we are. Not us on Mulberry Street. Not us
with the truth. Only rhythm and stupid singsong. Seuss, we never

learned from you. Off came our diapers but, being paupers,
we replaced them with newspapers. Long live the Lord

that loves guillotines. And long life to you! Reverend Jones
mixes his adieu. The 401 sleeps its epoch. Something wicked

this way comes—a hamster wheeling by, whistling odes to
reinforcements that go like this: *If we can't live in peace,*

then let's die in peace.

13.

Errors venerate the human factor. Like when love
becomes law, or when desire is supplied by the Nasdaq.

I tried to tell a man, *Things have affect* but all he said
was, *That's too much, man. Too much investment.*

Heart emoji! What's a safe space in the unsafe age,
all the implements in our hands drawing our blood

from the well? Memory mine and memory *it*: in the bed,
table, and cross-hatch is monstrous ability. Here Be Police

who eat explorers that touch too much. So, Mad Maxify.
Burn tires and string them on wires as dystopic signal,

a song of melted rubber and electricity as divine
connection to the electroned, our texts humming

the nacreous Ma Bell and her ill communication.
In the tire-fire sanctuary of dysphoria, don't suffer,

acknowledge. We'll give you a bed, cross-hatch,
and table. A tower too. Loosen the latches of trap doors

for cartoons who escape into claustrospaces with the call
of the killable: *let's self it.* Separate ways, unlatched

in the cross-hatch, Mad Max says: *I'm scared, Fifi. You know why?*
It's that rat circus out there, I'm beginning to enjoy it. Look,

any longer out on that road and I'm one of them, ya know?
A terminal crazy, except I've got a bronze badge that says

I'm one of the good guys. Mad Max and I, we yet sleep
the motion-sensed.

14.

Mama said there was an angel, but the angel's not for us.
She showed me the tin can, root, and dysphoric syllabus.

I tried to listen, I did, but the angel kept to itself.
Mama's slide-rule of doubt and fear was right.

Never fails. Not for us, but the smear of emotion
spreads the sky into pink-brown light as the sun collides

with atmospheric debris. Kaleidoscope me: black, black,
and Hadron black plus blue. Chromatograph, do as I say,

not as I do. Angel in the misguide, angel in the key,
angel in the horrible darkest part of *we*: singsong

playground and singsong bully, singsong in parliament
and singsong treaty, but shit never fails. Mama's angel

resists dumb elegies for the dead. It's not eternal life I want,
but the people I loved to be remembered, the hole in the head

to be filled. Call me Big Spender, call me a lout, give me
another slight to ruminate about. Cheque cashed. A baton

beans you in the noggin. My aim is true, I targeted you,
but officer—it was my cells, my genes, a coalesce

in the feeling-cloud: the death shroud. For my brother
Sammy, I turn it up loud and drive to the ends of the earth,

all in one night. We're Big Scare. We're Maglite.
We're frowny-faced guttersnipes that get all the girls.

We're jokers, all prowess and urge with curative purges
and binges on feeling as one piano key strikes—DDDD D   DDD, in me

and out of you. Flee.

15.

Can we refuse the door kicked in at night, or the stranger
sneaking into bed? We took the gutter by force and we

lasted all of an afternoon. The culvert routed us to the sand
flats, an affective frontier. We are queer to claim here.

Lookitme, lookitme, the estimated date of confinement of one
good feeling: gimme it in the chase, not in the stimulant hit

or the orderly's needle in the quelling ass. Again, Percy,
get whiskey-scratch and drop: *Tryin' to hold on to what he*

needs, he'd give up all his comfort. Sure. The floor is cool,
that much we know—like Mama's grave. Smooth, smooth

stone of St. Vincent de Paul. If you asked me how much I want
in this life, I'd say ALL. But ask first what I'd save, then what

I'd try to save. Come on down to the floor, constable, ask me
more. Query lust, love, the girl I didn't get, the one I did.

Percy, please advise the gutter masses: *trade the world*
for the good thing. Yes, yes, in the gutter I did as guttersnipes

do. Mama, we all said the same damn thing: be with me, wait
with me, stay with me, the men and the women and the angels

too. But the salt flats soliloquy is: *I gave you everything I had.*
The angels were the worst. Ashes are a bitter cast on the salt.

Who's at fault? If you hear me sing, it's with a mouth vacuum-sealed
on the floor, pressuring one incarcerated word: more. Percy, sing

backup? *Hold on to your precious love.* What if holding on
is the same thing as more, Percy? When a man loves a woman,

or a woman loves a man, we have a problem of excess in finite
containers: tin can, root, dysphoric syllabus. Mama said the angels

are not for us, and I ain't seen no angel except plucked,
on the way to the Dundas bus.

16.

See the plume, its black, cometous payload.
Strike the thought of release, of night-terrain,

of *Let us go.* Of *Please.* One nerve undulates.
Please breaks on the shore of more: smoke, hate,

the quiver of infliction, receipt, what falls awful
from the towered sky, what rises ragged from the earth.

Fire up all our black-and-whites: (1) Pain and no pain.
(2) Pain and pain and pain. (3) Dendrites: scalding blades

of grass that caress causalgic skin. The use of pain is plain.
It breaks our bones and calls us names. The life we had

becomes meaningful. We thank our god in screams.
The sun burns the sketchbook tinder. Motes coalesce

into representation of crowds and writhing-dark figures.
The temperature of the sun is aught, aught. The brightness

of the sun is aught, aught. A hand or eye placed against
the sun is aught, aught, and yet see the hands, the sun.

I have learned naught except burn paper from within. What lord
and what common, etched, drawn, thrown on the banks,

the bread is on fire. The transformation of seethe: the sun decides
to warm the bones of the Galileans. Friends, draw closer to the spit.

Fire makes the wall of white and water indistinguishable from body.
The closer a mote or a moth makes the journey, the vaster the void,

inadequate palette. Renounce the aught? *How much* is the aught,
How many are we is the aught. Naught in the belly and naught

in the sky, who are we to believe in why? There are many ways
of knowing, knowing the aught—and the car park looks on—

Charon, bring us news: another fisherman with proverbs.
If we can't live in peace, then let's die in peace.

PART TWO

Medical Inquiries and Observations Upon Diseases of the Mind

by Dr Benjamin Rush

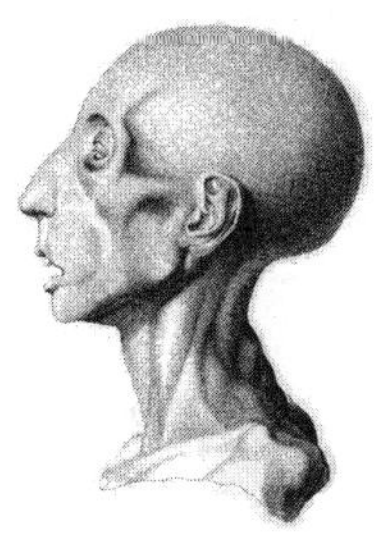

Preface of the experienced physician as patient

I know it is the defective head, rage within skin,
marrow sucked out of bones   and the harrowed hate
that grows within a sacculus   traded for guilt
the human enterprise reduced to a casual observer
who is mad   the head,   the head,
                              the doctor points to the head and says:

broken as the golden bowl be broken   or the pitcher be broken
at the fountain   or the wheel broken   at the cistern

broken as the toy is made to be broken, disposable in skyscraper
asylums and Super-Max jails and craft class, broken
as the lovers join in arms to be cleaved when the world insists
on therapeutic quiet   (pause) (pause) (pause) blam

broken accounts and broken redeemers,
broken in terms of failed dreamers,
broken itineraries of broc,
broken as I point at the ideal form,
my head in my hands

I diagnose the countenance as infallible proof of brokenness
I patent the cure of death masks and successful dreams
I call myself humble
I am made humble
the dreams make me humble
because the dreams leave me

How to Heal the Sick

Great care should be taken

Delusion's a straight
shot to god.
Do not deprive
the mad of it.
What man believes
partly relates to
what he wants
to believe. This
has everything to
do with treatment.
Because delusion is
a line connected
between two dear
points, do not break
the line. Instead,
redraw it by first
marvelling at the
line's elegance.

How to heal the sick with gaze

The countenance of a physician assists his eye,
accommodated to the state of the patient's conduct.

Your eye must establish government over patients afflicted
with mania. Your eye must see something to respect.

When you enter the cell of a deranged patient,
catch their  and look them out of their countenance.

Why? Apprentice, the dread of the eye is imposed
upon every beast. The tiger, mad bull, and enraged

dog all fly from it. A great effect is produced by
looking the patient out of countenance. Vary your aspect

from the highest sternness to mildest benignity and play
keys in the eye: a grave countenance checks the frothy

levity of a deranged patient in an instant just as a placid
one chases away his gloom. A stern look puts a stop

to garrulity, and cheerfulness extorts smiles even from
the face of melancholy itself. Your eye forests the beasts.

But do not rely upon the eye alone—also use bleeding.

Prescription for bloodletting

Blood vessels flow to a meridian sun.
All mariners go there in time. Float,
hold the clotting platelets as flotsam.

Be seated on the brain where blood
satisfies solar constraints. Arterial
disease makes men morbid and irregular,
suffering sense-fullness, head pain,
wakeful red eyes such as precede fever,
high coloured, and pulse natural as to frequency.

Natural as to frequency is the leached
pulse and black purgatives I teach.
Blood pours from the haemorrhoidal seat.

I make men pale and faint. They cease
to perfuse brains with blood, so as to settle
their fulsome cerebrums. Why not act heroic
where it hurts? Leech the head until
it bursts, blood reduced to fat sheens
that gulp great draughts from veins.

Natural as to frequency is viscous sleep
madmen never had, but treatment
seizes them to its bosom until comatose.

I bleed them, and they speak of leeching in dreams.

Ongoing notes on bloodletting

(1) Be copious on the first attack of the disease, 20 to 40 ounces of blood taken at once unless fainting is induced before that quantity is drawn.

(2) The patient must be bled in a standing posture.

(3) Bleed them not only when the pulse is morbid. In the presence of good pulse yet provided great wakefulness, redness in the eyes, a ferocious countenance, and noisy and refractory behaviour, still bleed them.

(4) The quantity of the blood drawn should be greater than in any other disease. Cures can come through the accidental loss of large quantities of blood. Many mad people who have attempted to destroy themselves by cutting their throats have been cured by the profuse haemorrhages which have succeeded those acts. Several instances have occurred within my knowledge.

(5) Apply cups to the temples, behind the ears, and to the nape of the neck. Use the wet method, with a lancet to bring the blood out.

(6) If the gentler method of wet cupping fails, add leeches for the same purpose and to the same places.

(7) In persons subject to the piles, apply leeches to the haemorrhoidal vessels. The sympathy of the brain with these vessels is so intimate that the disease yields as readily to the loss of blood from them.

Gyrater

Swing and see-saw are the wrong kind of motion.
Rotary settles the blood, forces it to flow against
its flow and move where it should move.
Rotary embraces the blood with a feint, reducing
small minorities of capillaries into beds to reroute
the arterial shock. Forgive the blood that knows not
what it does. The rotary makes vascular beds
and sluices blood out, draining blood past the pan
and back into the old and good body where it is set
free though I know the blood wishes to return
to where it loves. But look at this woman, her face
pulled against the wooden board, her hands and legs
in the anatomical position. Eenie meenie mind
go twitch, don't stop Gyrater until 100 revolutions
finish. Covered in vomit and throat outscreamed,
a great and strong wind rent the mountain. Distance
returns from its centre of motion, effect measured
by the pulse. Prove thy servants, give us pause
natural as to frequency.

Bartholin speaks in high terms of what he calls 'flagellation' in certain diseases

In mentioning the cures performed by the whip
(and do not forget leeches and cups), I equip

this degrading wisdom: the man who is bent,
tied, and bleeding first heard the chirrup-word

of home. He thought he could love a wife
and be free. He wanted otherwise. Now,

here with me, I must wield the lash to lacerate skin
with sense. I turn out lights to kindle childhood

fears, keeping the door closed to remind him
of where he'd escape. There is no plea anyone

can hear for things to be well. Inside and outside,
we suffer transient spells. He has a cell, a bed,

and a morbid face. Only when stroked does he know
thresholds, madness, and the world. The whip marks

the man with time. As each blow hits, I drone: *I smite*
thee with madness, blindness, and astonishment of heart.

Conversions of parts suppressing secrets, becoming a sharer
inside oneself, emerging paroled into truth and light.

I pick different fights. It curls like a serpent around my neck,
the man before me outstripped, his skin welted in pain,

held as in shale or amber, stranger again.

There is a method of taming refractory ~~horses~~ patients

Prevent the old and good body from lying down
or sleeping by the thrust of sharp pointed nails
into the ~~horse's~~ patient's flank for three days
and nights.

(Conjurors profess an art of distraction:
magic the *occasion*, not the *cause*)

As constant exertion of muscles supporting
the body results in debility, pain induced in
muscles attracts the morbid brain's attention,
relieving primary disease. For some, a threat
to tear up a picture of their bride suffices;
others require the threat to burn a letter.
Some need the temperature lowered and
clothes removed. Others need to tame
refractory horses with nails.

In Aberdeen, I once witnessed an unusual
method used by a layman: a number of madmen
yoked in a plough, compelled by fear and force
to furrow the fields.

One with the froth and another hearing voices,
another mute even when lashed, the largest brute
filthy with food-stains, each man hirsute. When
yoked, they act as a team of oxen who move the blade
deeply. The farmer who beat them as beasts sang hymns,
his infrequent speaking voice the fear and the rod his chancel.

The Sick Sing

Phrenetic dispositions

Madness is to delirium what walking in sleep is to dreaming.

Men walk the hospital asleep and enraged with faulty reasonings.

They suffer the frontal Babel.

Locked in the phrenetic disposition, susceptible to death if wakened, their nerves are predisposed to drown from song.

Orchestration of blows, a great tide against a cracked barrier—where these men are and what they see, they will only sing. Give them pens.

The death-hymn of the prisoner

In the jail of Philadelphia, a notorious offender composed ludicrous verses in his head. After several silences, he asked

for a pen:

All ye who carry a shield for those who hunt the wounded or heal
them in taverns and brothels and cancel the love of life parcelled
in chambers of heart and the constitution to stay in the love of life,

sing.

Sing by day when the shield is for slings and arrows;
sing by night when the shield is a roof to crawl underneath,
though the love of life is singing underneath, never any shields.
Sing to the remains of the excitement of the system awakened
by fever and pain that take refuge in the mind.

Tristimania

Cures of patients, who suppose themselves to be glass, may easily be performed by pulling a chair, upon which they are about to sit, from under them, and afterwards showing them a large collection of pieces of glass as the fragments of their bodies.

—Dr Benjamin Rush

Tinted windows of the killer's Camaro burnished windows of the Wall Street skyscraper bulletproof windows of the Popemobile stained-glass window made in my grandfather's name (gold makes the wine-red colour) window-face of my father's watch cracked glass in the parking lot shards in the park sandbox encasement of light in bulb substrate of the looking glass. Look at my history:

I fancied of glass, first my fingers and then arms. Once translucent, I let the doctor see through me: using a candle, he saw my glass heart, liver, and spleen. He diagnosed an error in furnace: I was fired imperfectly, I should return to flesh and begin again. He was right: I wanted to die. Before I agreed, I asked first about impurity: why conduit light when grit and bark prevent perfect images? He said: fall, break, and you shall be made flesh again. He pushed my chest and I shattered on the ground.

How I see: through eyes of glass that are painted and then burnt intact. How I feel: through the silica whorls daguerreotyped on fingertips. I love the cold texture of my thick limbs, and on my brittle lips are light hymns. I am invisible except as intensification of light that glows past bits of dirt. The doctor is blinded when he looks, he holds hands over his eyes that are also glass, but he is afraid to become an entire eye, a pane.

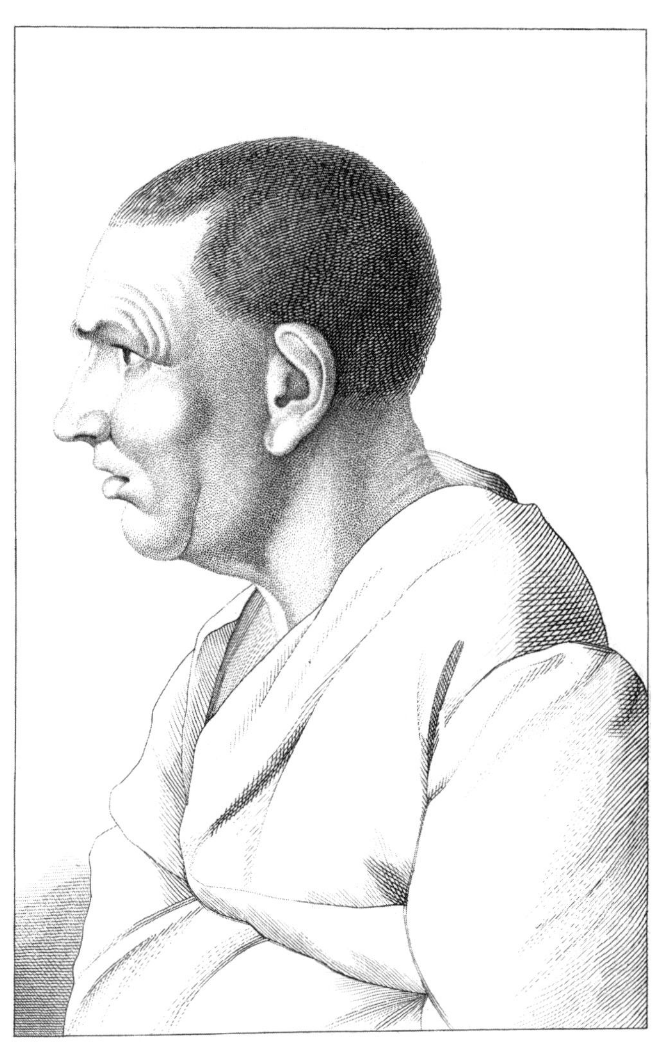

Note from a bachelor with tristimania

Whosoever born alone will die alone. Whosoever reduced
to dreams of the mother's breast is meant to later sit at my right hand
and sing of the broken latch. Whosoever wished to see the world
from the father's shoulders will look at the sky from a deathbed of
grass and wonder if this, too, is what *he* saw. Whosoever wanted wisdom
will have this word instead: solus. Whosoever makes prescriptions
will not be included in my book of judgements. Whosoever lies down
with angels will be consecrated in me, and in my name your line will die out
on the earth with the selfsame disease: aloneness. Whosoever gives
alms to the sick, understand: alms disappear in the molten eyes
of the mother with her goodbyes or past the cracked rasp of the father
and his claws on the tablets or scattered by the angels who fell
to keep you company and give children until I called the winged back
to me to watch their mortal children die alone. The stone-father
and the milk-mother and the choired angels and the fetid light are whosoever.
They precede, whosoever. They agree, whosoever. They love, whosoever.
Whosoever born alone will die alone, it's all I want you to know.

The doctor's opinion on irrigation in this case of tristimania

He believes that by discharging the contents of his bladder,
he shall drown the world.

He believes it to be a glass case that ferments his waste,
siphoning the metal salts required for stained-glass windows.

He believes he may turn into glass and his urine will not flow.

Written in his notebook is this beautiful evidence:

Angels course into silver nitrate for halos, use cousin's rose
for Christ's flesh tones. The image of a saint or dove erupting
into silver nitrate and fixed with fire: I shall drown the world
in stain … there was a flood, waters rose in punishment to drown
the cousins of man and beast. With silver nitrate I'll pepper
doctor's beard and fix his face in glass, see his mind as symbol.

He believes his urine will drown Philadelphia though he cannot fill
a chamber-pot. He dances and holds it as long as he can.

I tell him: irrigate the flowers and the grasses, water the ditches
and farms, bring down the dust. And lo, he does, but his riposte
is all our sacrums are crucifixes.

Dr Morely's written account of a boy at Naples, for years

This state of derangement when completely formed appears in the body
as walking with a quick step, or standing still, or running on the spot,
often with the hands and eyes elevated towards the heavens,

or the hands beating the breast or the hands slapping the face

or the hands clapping or a fist into an open hand;

the attack of chairs and tables with white-knuckled hands;

rocking with the hand cocked, striking the head upon stone;

a smile about to lasso the face, or a mouth sucking inside a hand;

ears that erupt from the head as if from the brow of Zeus, auricles
as Athena, hands that held only themselves;

skin peeled back from lips, fingertips,

frenzied dance with hands attentive to no partner.

Letters to Dr Rush from an escaped man, who was so happy in his paroxysms of madness, that when he was well he longed with impatience for their return

Everyone is too slow,
I know this, and yet
I am the same speed.

My feeling is that I
never lived, except
to long like an opium-
eater for some other
state, a behind-place
one reverts to with
draught-closed eyes.

With no sane topics
except beauty and
appetite, I have the
window to watch
the languid summer
waste into fall.

Outdoors, a
petticoated
throng ambles
in the afternoon.

*

Doctor Rush, have you stared at the sky and convinced other men of its incomparable configuration, forcing whole crowds to look up at midday at unmarked blue? Doctor Rush? Am I speaking too fast again? I'll do as you taught me—emphasize every word.

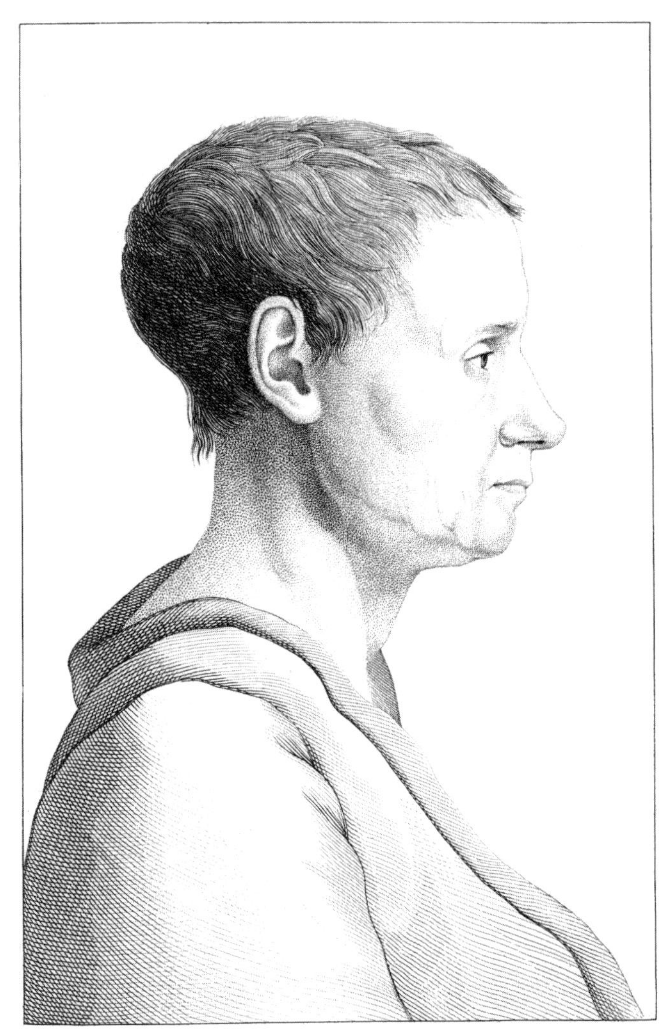

When will I change?

Who wouldn't choose beauty and appetite?

The sky is on offer for all.

Women are happiest when closest to fire.

To fly, to see the shapes moving no one else can see, to hear a voice in my head, to move objects with the gravity of my eyes, to flee from my house and live, whole continents turning and locked in rancid professoriats of commerce? Every word, every word, emphasize, every word, every word, emphasize, I can change, emphasize.

Who doesn't want to be free?

*

The professional secret of longing is this:

as

children

we

were

hurt,

we

can

never

get

far

enough

away.

The eldest son of a Scotch nobleman had great piety

A man can be predisposed to madness in the most trifling causes

He died of disease

A few weeks after the consummation of the eldest son's
worldly prospects by marriage to a most amiable young lady

He died of disease

that son felt like he won a high prize in a lottery of exhaust
as if he had refused to say grace to his maker every mortal second
of his life, his wife looking on him as if she were happy but

He died of disease

he could never meet her gaze, she being the high prize he could never
redeem in his own self   That eldest son preferred sitting by the window.
He spoke to me of great love   I leeched his tongue seeking to correct
the fundamental problem of blood-vessels   That night, the leeches sated,

He died of disease

his wife made her way to Pennsylvania Hospital for emergency counsel
Such evidence that blood-vessels enthrone men upon the seat of madness!
She confessed that the marriage was yet unconsummated   *Would leeches
help him make love to me?* While she was gone, the eldest son of a Scotch
nobleman took my treatment too close to heart and opened his veins arid

He died of disease

Death is the effect of derangement in all such cases.

But madness is excited in the understanding most frequently by impressions that act primarily upon the heart

I.

Grief induced madness in Hannah Lewis, formerly a patient who in distress produced, in the prisoners of the town of Liège, exquisite delicacy while ministers of state and generals of armies languished their lives with the loss of one eye, by an affray in a country tavern, which materially affected Hannah's beauty.

An American Indian, in consequence of seeing his looking glass soon after its recovery from a violent attack of the Once Beautiful Lady Mary Wortley Montagu (herself ashamed in looking) too was unable to bear the mortifying contrast between the two extremes of her life, colonized and 'free'. Lady Mary explained that 'hundreds face insane consequences of money, but oftener among the rich, who only lose a part of their property, than among persons in moderate circumstances, who lose their all. So it is with the vain and beauty.'

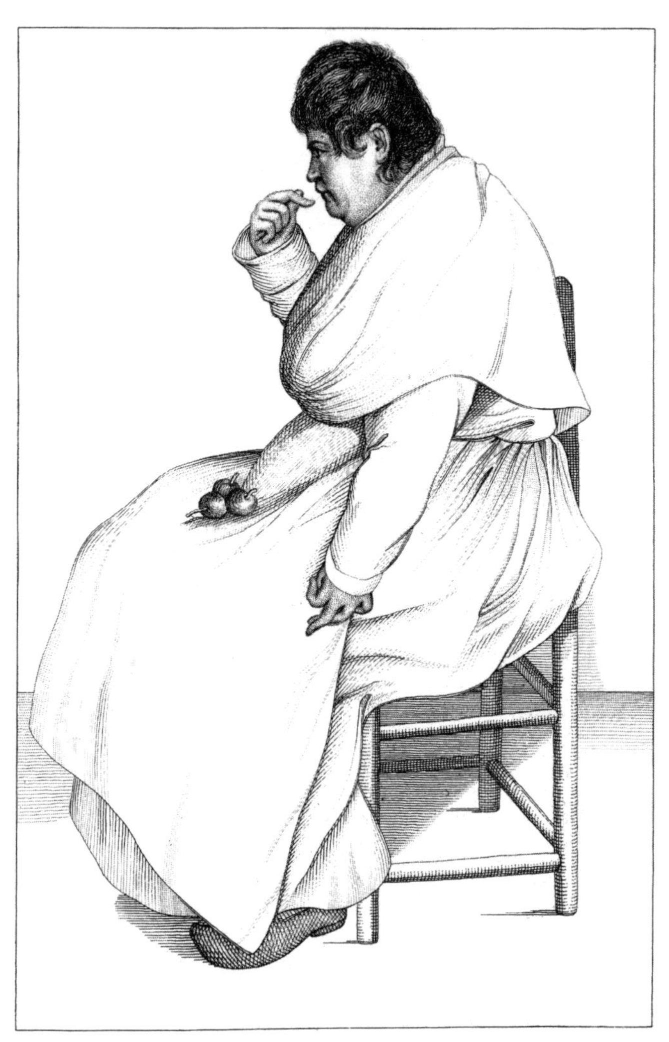

II.

the eyes reappear
as the perpetual star
of empty disorder
that takes pleasure
in the never-trick.
Pass on emotion
springing like lightning
from limb to limb.
Light ancient straw
ignored by horses
and watch stars
ignite in the field,
St. Lawrence entering
the barn with shield
(never any shields)
his head turned
to the hottest corner,
straw in his mouth.

Cowper sends Dr Rush an introductory letter outlining the particulars of his case

I, Cowper, slake thirst with the body
of the lake of fire, to fear one iamb
that becomes a hymn and makes
mystery out of the feeling that washes
my brain, oh rant and rave and register
of the grave, stone and blessed storm
with foot planted in the norm of brimstone
gods and recidivist grace, all the men poets,
all the men in their place, no Mary to love
and no Mary to have, the Olney curate
gone and my amazements sampled alone.

Sex is best with widows, their imaginations
reduced to sitting on sofas, timepiece
in hand; or taking walks in the garden
on winter evenings and winter mornings,
a noose thrown 'round the highest hymn
at noon, raptures of my composition
conjured up to serve cups that cheer
but not inebriate. I will die damned
below Judas, more abhorred than he
and not insane for money, but for the
preference of an end to suffering
over everlasting life.

Dr Burton recommends, in the highest terms, the reading of the Bible to hypochondriac patients like Christopher Smart

Christopher Smart once stood
from prayer, never to see his
children again. Midsummer,
his mood high and disorganized,
he kneeled on a London street
to feel the broken stone bite
his prayer. He rose to watch
commoners seek pleasures
that he too had been ruined
by. He saw men and women
walking undisturbed, as if the
world were still the same—
but it was not. He took Samuel
Johnson's shoulder and pulled
him into the street. Falling upon
his knees, tearing his trousers,
Smart chanted, *Let us pray.*

Seatonian Prize Poem I

—Asylum, Kilingsbury, Northhamptonshire

I once looked at Anna Maria
and felt a field, unchanging
in winter, the small animals
preserved underground or in
trees. I walked the frozen

estate looking for Anna Maria
again and couldn't find her
yet I knew she was here,
would always be here,
I do not need to see her
to know

                                        and though
under dense ice and impenetrable
earth, beyond thick bark, past my
eyes are a thousand lives that wait
for the crackingly sudden resumption
of life. Such waiting I make for my
wife. I do not need to see her to wait.

Beauteous the moon full on the lawn,
and beauteous, when the veil's withdrawn,
the wife to her spouse; beauteous the asylum
deck'd and fill'd, when to heav'n of heav'ns
the men here build our heart-directed vows.

Goodness is dissolution: Anna Maria,
my life was high, too many abominable
nights away from the estate. Goodness
still! All is goodness. Even with rash
purchases and drink you know I was true,
that the fields I wandered were yours.
Nightly, the visitor comes to windows
of the impenitent while I sing psalms
of my own composing.

Here

there is no god who holds my hand
and leaves me awed; prayers come
hard and bare. I am hidden. I only
wanted you. Madness reduces me
to poems. We had two children who
yet sleep in a field, buried in ice where
you yield no change. I am alone, my
prayers unremembered by rough-cut
stone that hosted my knees, my cries
for you the same, the same. Anna Maria,
when I die, I'll finally pray. Your name.

Mon homme

After *Portrait of a Man Suffering From Delusions of Military Command*, 1822, by Théodore Géricault

Call this monomania:

Leaves of grass in the field,
all the yield signs held high,
and no other campaign:

reign, reign, reign. I ran
from nightmare fields,
carried by the leaves of grass,

condemned not to be believed.
We are all going to die.
Is that proof enough of mind?

I stare at the military wall,
the tents with their orders,
the charge soon to come.

I bequeath this likeness
to the ones who don't know
the war is over,

who also don't know
we have so little time together.
Take aim.

i sing the body electrocuted

For Robert Dziekanski

Lands of Odysseus, of cracked covenants and tyrannies of lovers—all serve god metaphors.

Trade anger for knowledge to not understand.

There is no technology to my bond or words.

I make no promise except that I am confused.

I'm wearying of inquiry.

Is the one flesh one?

Has it always been?

It remains cold, in need of touch.

Are you human?

If so, I don't understand … and am happy, for I sing the body electrocuted.

The song starts as this lie: control understands.

But do not understand.

Coo, sing, smile.

Take your pick of the myth-kitty and leverage old stories against
the new.

Send your Odysseus-equivalent as procedure into the future where he'll
be as baffled as you are, as your flesh will always be.

Try to not understand his fear as you reach for your belted bolts of
lightning and strike the formidable Law.

His pained cells cry out something you can't understand.

As you lie of process and procedure, Odysseus dies.

He sings the body electrocuted, a song in which death is never safe.

We are the ones to carry the dead, to make myths of the dead, and to
carry their myths.

His message is one we can only hope to not understand, in the least
violent way.

Sing, my ill brothers and sisters, of holding charge in the body!

The ur-myth renders Truth as a stunned and furious walk past
the Certain.

Be as a battery to the sun.

Self-Diagnosis

Prognostications of the Good Doctor

1. Persons who have children are more difficult to cure than those who are childless.

2. Madness resulting from lesions of the brain is seldom cured.

3. Madness which succeeds epilepsy is always incurable.

4. Intractable madness arises from the revival of old and dormant passions, especially when that passion is love or grief.

5. Love which causes madness does not revive with its cure.

By means of torture, inflicted from pious, but superstitious motives by some priests

In Rome, an instance of chronic madness cured by trepanning priests
from a dirty church who rubbed the bore-hole and the battered skull together.

Are you blind, O priests, to the confounding hand of God moving your hand?
From the Gospel of Randomized Controlled Trial: *as every man hath received*

the gift, beloved, think it not strange concerning the fiery ablation, as though
some strange thing happened to you. As every man hath been given a gift

and as some gifts can't be seen, I touch my own head, plug the blowhole
of the dead, the trephine gone

but the priests looking on.

Dr Rush dreams of his wedlock

train of wedding dress and train of engine,
the sleep with cold feet and Julia in my arms,
white apparition and the blood in my brain,
aura of pinprick and scintilla and scotoma
and sleep that night that came after I broke
her open, a train that follows behind the odd
waves set loose from Gyrater

and alive on top, alive and inside, alive
with my arm pinning hers, the muscular action
inducing a transient delirium, the dream, sleep
behaviour disorder and acting the dream inside
out, an act of release my arm sending waves down
the train, the blood disordered and going

Prevent the evils that might arise from a mistake of this kind

The doctor left Pennsylvania Hospital in love,
saying he wanted his family again. For a year
he sat staring at water, wanting to drown.
My head, he said, *is the closest I come to burial.*

Making sense to himself and eating alone,
he resisted the treatments he taught me:
Gyrater, bleedings. We agree: the inconsolable
need treatment, but the physician must heal himself.

Near the end, he surfaced to ask for his wife.
He sang departure songs to those who heard
voices and claimed the voices sang like a choir
of angels. At the last, this consolation:

the madness of fellowship with the mad.
I heard him outside, the walls thrumming
with his song, his baritone wrapping around
the hospital stone as matrix. His muscles

disused, the best visiting consultants agreed
on his chronic case. Have you heard a doctor
say, 'Incurable?' It sounds like laughter from
a star. The look on his face was as if grippe

had crushed his lips into lines and stretched
them out into a harmonica of delusion. Near
the end, he asked for dispatch. I summoned
Mrs Rush. When he saw her, he rose and held

her in his arms. Though he was thin, it was she
who fainted when he sang the natural-as-to-frequency:

> *Natural as to frequency the wine-dark eyes*
> *become anemic, the black blood sapped.*
> *Natural as to frequency the snowed tongue,*
> *overgrown from lack, has its field prepared.*
> *Natural as to frequency the urine diminishes*
> *to whey-coloured trickles when I bleed them,*
> *natural as to frequency the pulse beaten back*
> *from an insane meridian when I bleed them,*
> *I bleed them down to bradycardic sanity. Too bled*
> *to move, too bled to think past the boundaries*
> *of their exhaustion, the proof of my theory is there—*

Love seeks its out, no matter the dysmorphisms
of time. She took him home. On the night of discharge
he drank strychnine, arriving back at Pennsylvania
Hospital in an incurable posture. As he writhed, she said,

> *He stared at the walls and sang of shields until he got hoarse.*
> *Never any shields, never any shields, never any shields—*

The Good Doctor Signs Off on the Case

On the anatomy table I once extracted
a message embedded deep in a chest,
posterior to the heart, anterior to the spine:

'We are so selfish that if the resurrection power were lodged in our hands, we should immediately run to the graves of our dear departed, and fetch them.'

When placed on the scale,
the message had no weight.

I lost my father when I was six years old.

I do not want him.

It is my own self I grieve.

In his final year, Louis XIV was 76.
With gangrene spreading from his feet,
the Sun King recited Psalm 70:

Domine, ad adjuvandum me festina.

There is a different message
in me to be cut out, a message
as rigid as my body.

Students, wield your atlases without
tears and place my body in genuflection.
I die composed in your company.

The psalm of anatomy tables: I hope
the sufferings of our fellows from causes
mentioned may find relief by the attention
of students who grieve their own selves.

I turn you back! I'm weightless.

Self-Diagnostic Soliloquy

So cold
in the dark,
so cold.

We wanted
to be free,
but we're cold.

Once the question
Where are you
was warm.

But it cooled
in the air.
Where, where, where—

Cousin to *why,*
why, why.
How to be free?

How to be
is the
question of cold.

Ho ho ho.
Brr, merry motherless!
We can't breathe.

We can't think
the crumbling rampart,
the mowed field.

No. We feel dysphoric,
Heraclitus sinking chest-deep
in the Portobello.

He moves deeper—
grief's a
temperature of image.

Emotion is sonic.
Poetry expends shrill
blasts. Better lives!

Why be concerned
about why or
where? Rest. Be.

Come.
Follow
me.

PART THREE

Pain on a One-to-Ten Scale

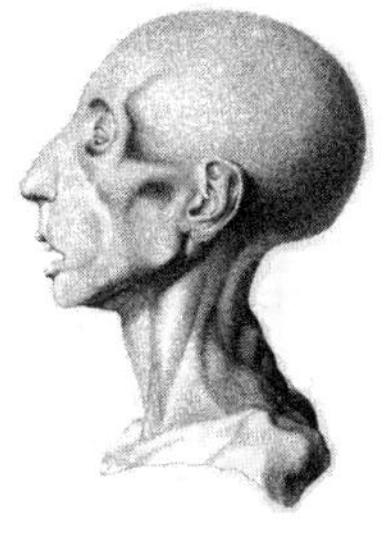

Earth, Fire, Air, Water

The cry of pain is life —Bichat

Feel your cells.

They dwell in the drama you set,

that spell of forget and remember.

Cells are demented elephants,

atolls that move in storms.

Heaven or hell is the Brownian motion.

From the sky: portents and weather, the impetus.

In Hooke's eye, pain is an organelle.

Cells die together, as do we.

En masse, the telos is alone,

yet,

for me, that's never true.

I will die thinking of you. I will die thinking.

Of you, the pain says nothing. You are.

What I say, and sing, for I am in pain,

and have always been: *I am alive.*

Pain is not the cry.

The cry is that I think of you,

I think of life.

Ripley's Aquarium

I.

I wish I were less; and lesser I shall be.
My son and I stand on a conveyance.
The fish neither single file nor school,
but arranged as coral accumulative—
as death dispersed, shard-hardened.
Motion scrapes the transparent glass.
He likes the stingrays. Me, my mind's not right.
Other families *oooh* and *ahhh*—what luck.
My son and I, we're silent; he sees electric
as I fight the urge, as always, to close my eyes.

II.

Less about me: the boy's not happy,
exactly; he's quiet, a synapse underwater,
Cousteau leaking red. He's heard my sonar try
to track how far a thing is from having—
he knows. Too far. And smiles more than I,
and therefore becomes this address. What eloquence!
Why fight some full fathom of greater sense?
The water never moves, saying, *Choose life and die.*
A straight line, those two. My son and I.

III.

I wish I were less; less I shall be.
Why don't the sharks eat everything?
Each question sparks against a glass.
Deep, strange green—a snow globe zoo.
I wish I could sing like Leviathan rising,
shake the scene and cue the dirge—
but my eyes are closed. Oh, I don't know the words.
The crowd will not celebrate. Pain is deafness here,
the vacuumed chamber, butterflies affixed.
My son looks on, suddenly sad.
I know, I say. We don't choose.

In Each

In each of your cries is: 'I'm alone.'
We are. I learned first in pain;
the poor man's wisdom. Again, it comes; again,
and you'll be lost, grown up,
heart gone brutal from the fare:
but first, on your mother's arm, take special pains
to feel just what cost she carries
when she carries your weight. She buries
the oncoming fear. My dear, it keeps us sane!
And underneath it all is, 'I'm alone.'
I can't save you, or take the cry and make it go away.
It's true. And don't stay clear—
the pain's your own, your name. Speak
it when most lost; perhaps I'll find you.

In the SERT Room

Cameras bathe the playground. When he was born:
milk and terror, a knot in the cord that severed.
Hospitals. Referrals of steed. How to be alone.
Pre-ambulance. Some awful sound that authenticates
the human, a drone from the lower world,
a beast climbing rung by rung:

Ohhhhhhhhhhhhahhhhhhhhhwwwwwwww.

Delayed abecedaries, numerologies, and procedures of art.
I port love from crayons. My son the native, a primitive,
has reconnaissance from where the butcher lives.
He sees where we go and he tells me this:

Ohhhhhhhhhhhhhhahhhhhhhhhwwwwwwwww.

By day, he sits in a chair. In his mind are bent lines—
the residue of the other place. I wish he'd sail out to sea
and tell the horizon of love. (That's what I do.)
One night, at the boundary, I whispered

Ohhhhhhhhhhhhhhahhhhhhhhhwwwwwwwww

in his ear. Translation: *do not range too far.*
He came back and we played cars, trucks, and blocks.
Emotion is my reason—him. We two are of the world
and we are not. We understand the soul. Institutions order
life as ruse. We have only each other, we can only fail
each other, the system and me. He tells me this:

Ohhhhhhhhhhhhhhahhhhhhhhhwwwwwwwww

I need not learn again. For the floor and to keep score
I scream out iambs in fervour, our little time together
spent disorganized on the carpet, our faces in love,
each metric tick-tock my warning for the coming beast,
who must come.

The Day My Son Seized for 27 Minutes, I Wished on a Villainous Star

Another life? Yes. Fuck you.
How far away we are—
doesn't matter. Fuck you.

Afar, he sees what he sees. He's slow.
He's my son. This means war.
Another life? Yes. Fuck you.

He drools as report card. Drools and drools.
I want him back from Charon.
Doesn't matter? Fuck you.

One day I wiped my hand across his brow.
Demon, begone! I commanded. He drooled stars.
Another life? *Yes.* Fuck you.

That my heart wants to kill this misfortune
doesn't matter. That my heart is sore
doesn't matter. Fuck you.

Armamentarium: waiting, left lateral decubitus,
medicines, and faith lost on the radar for
another life? Yes. *Fuck you*
doesn't matter? Fuck you.

Air Prophecies for the Bride

Is it hands I feel that beat the breast
to bring the voice? I don't know. Who
has the choice to know? The summons
was my skin, whatever room I was in,
away from where you were, in fields
or free. The secret counsel that tells me
what I know quietens when your face
appears. You were three years old then.
How fair is want? How fair—

dear, we're all in love with one another.
It's fair we go to hell, fair we die, fair
we tell each other fairy tales, fair Father
played peekaboo in hospitals as you grew.

If love was true then, I wouldn't be me
and you wouldn't be you, half on the
ground and half in the air. Understand:
struck letting go is a command—

on your wedding day: no medical
hypotheses will explain brains to poems
or poems to brains, nor love to love.
Medicine cannot make rhyme
ring through the chains on your legs
or arms because prophecy is not fair
for you, but true love is.

How will it go for you? Dad's golden rule
condemns: do as I say, not as I do. Forget
the frozen countenance of long ago and far
away, some common horror of how your
parents found one other. Remember more
the half-in-air.

Saints preserve all diagnoses because
they cannot preserve us. How alien
we are when most alone! What fire
will warm us when we've been bad
and all we have is used? What charm
remains for use when the voice fails,
when skin can't muster pleasure to flood
manifold pain?

I don't know.

How fair is it that I've never known,
yet the inapplicables of death will touch
your laugh. The voice says: *lack*
of hypothesis means the hypothesis
is lack. Why yes—my brain will never
be as close to a girl of three as when
on shoulders or in arms I had half
an idea that you were you. There's no
choice in that feeling, there's just you.

May he find you forever like I found you
then, still half-in-air.

Given

The secrets of losing recede until regret
is the only expression: instruct in error,

in the luck that flung you into wonder.
I've held you evenings in a briarpatch,
spitting lullabies that permit a temporary claim.

Song of diamond, ease, mortal wound, the shared cry
that you were never mine as I am not yours.

Fathers distinguish love's night terrors from dreams,
years on. Your own girls will long
for bedtime stories, and you too will spill
the secret I'm trying to tell: our feelings are *am,*

what will be. By day we play, are hurt within
protectorates of choice. I can't choose.
You were given to me. To lose.

Not Long Ago

Refuse the song, refuse the silence, and hear the march instead.
Hoofbeats mark the dead: I woke to find the house infected,
the girl who loved horses

(there's a mare black and shining)

nowhere near, as close as her room. The boy convulsed in bed.
Both in fields of ash. My son collapsed with each failed touch,
my daughter graced masks. If on the face of the dead erupts
a wish to be remembered and forgiven, then O lord

I have seen that face prepared!

That face contorts, its lips rip up as eyes deviate left—
the compass for joy. I love my little boy: in my lap,
a tattered stick.

Fathers of the sick want alms for the sick. Fuck useless song.
I left the cross. I had to leave. I capered for the betterment of elements,
a boy shattered on the floor with a girl fixed on the lance.
Joy is hurled like bolts from the blue to hit children
according to the most beautiful rule: love kills the good

(I heard there was a secret chord)

to take blood from his mouth, no sound from her mouth
so crystalline by salt. Now they're guarded by horses of ash
that course in fields.

Resilience Trait

A long line extends from the rifle, saw,
and hoe. They, the valleyed ones

with violence and will—they showed
me I could die. I didn't always know.

Did you? Oh. Skin's like this: in a second,
you can't feel. Infinity comes on its own

count. So record with this different line:
secret feeling that kills if you look

at it straight, just like all the other killers.
With the resilience trait, your hardy strain

is neither start nor end, but some middle
hell of long pain and short escape. Who

communicates gaps as the trait skips
from knowledge to knowledge? Pretend

the worst is when the line connects,
when the trait fails and you've got sense

to thank for realizing, too late, you were wrong.
The line was always too long and straight,

pointing to the dead who point to the dead.

What My Father Told Me

Our children cannot save us. They are meant
to burn us on pyres. Dancing at midnight, they
convulse in glee. The inheritance is: they fight
to be free so as to be scared again. But who will
remember to douse the pit? Who becomes an
authority on pain? Under moonlight the fire
stays hot and no one learns how long fuels last.
We forget in fun. Shane, it burns only so the trace
of fathers and mothers are black and the corpse
of what made us won't hijack a child's full-throated
shriek at ceremonial flames. We need names, my son,
we need our names to do work we cannot do—
to burn nobly. Look, what else do you need?
I taught you to spell it like I taught you to bleed.

Angelic Salutation

1.

Out of ether, halothane, and drugged-down
brain-sate they gave me q.i.d.—I rose to meet
my mother in the afternoons. The ceiling
in carousel blur and then her, a blue dress
in a chair. The blent psychiatric air: I opened
my eyes, and she was there. The ruminant
hospital gave me to her, or her to me: knocked
down in thought, shackled in act, she didn't care.
She waited for me every inpatient day.
She could leave. I had to stay.

2.

Now she's infected and almost dead. In the ICU,
bedridden, tubes enter her head two-by-two.
Drains snake from her belly cut transverse
and wide. What does she have inside? A *me* once
long ago, but now internal burns from the purulent
burst. I felt such stellated abuse in my nerves once
when I wanted, but now I don't want the worst.
I want her eyes to rise up and escape the drug clenched
arteries and opiates dousing an incredible fire.
Watching the brute air shoved into her lungs,
I wait by the bed in a chair positioned for her
to see, should she, my face asking for the honest
lively rise of what was always inside.

3.

The priest came to the hospital. He invited me
to mass's scorch. This too shall pass; there shall
be weeping and gnashing of teeth as human law.
As the priest talked, she chomped on the tube.
Oil dripped from her eyes. I said, 'Father, yes.
It has been a lifetime since my last.' On Sunday
at St. Vincent de Paul, her pew empty, the church
full of the old, the sick, and the small, I crossed
my chest on this sixth Sunday of Easter, Jesus
splayed on the wood, Mary standing on the earth.
Floating in drug-space or face in the dirt, who
chooses their faith, and what is it worth? In supportive
delirium, do we pray with our bodies bent over the bed?
Do the dead recognize the dead? Do we genuflect
to prove we can yet stand? I stood in the aisle, following
the communion line. Hands clasped in front, I took
the bread. On my mouth, the body for my body
dissolved and was gone: mother's hand, her step,
or her dress in an old chair. I walked past Mary's
statue. She wore a blue robe. Father Weir chanted
to God as I mouthed a refrain.

4.

In the hospital of no soul's address,
of monitors, lines, infinite regress,
common now and at the hour of my mother,
the hour of ordinary Sundays and ordinary song.
Forget the fasts of Lent. Who kept for you?
Index drowning in the fount, I sing:
who calls us back to ourselves?

The air bed's circulatory roar pushes past the wake.
Angels come to ground, custodians sweeping
the tile with stone hair. A chart scatters
the message of name. We pray with our bodies
in the language of pain.

Sources

The cover image, *Théodore Géricault (1791–1824) Dying*, (1824, oil on canvas), is by Alexandre Correard, (1788–1857) / Musee des Beaux-Arts, Rouen, France / Bridgeman Images.

All interior images are courtesy of the Thomas Fisher Rare Book Library, the University of Toronto, from *Des maladies mentales* (Paris: J.-B. Baillière, 1838) by Jean-Étienne-Dominique Esquirol (1772–1840).

Medical Inquiries and Observations Upon Diseases of the Mind. Dr Benjamin Rush. Philadelphia: Kimber and Richardson, 1812.

The Mourner: or, The Afflicted Relieved (5th ed). Dr Benjamin Grosvenor London: George Keith, 1765.

'To Consumption' from *The Remains of Henry Kirke White, With an Account of His Life.* Vol. II. Ed. Robert Southy. London: W. Wilson, 1807.

Every day spent growing up in the text of New Brunswick

Acknowledgements

Thanks to my editors and friends.

Poems from this volume have appeared in the following journals: *Event, Fiddlehead, filling Station, Literary Review of Canada Matrix* and *Rampike.*

Some poems also appeared in *We Need Our Names* (Toronto: Anstruther Press, 2014).

'Not long ago' appeared in the anthology *Translating Horses* (London, Ont.: Baseline Press, 2015).

A version of 'Note from a bachelor with tristimania' will appear in *Tag: Canadian Poets at Play* from Oolichan Books.

Part I of this book was shortlisted for the 2016 *Seattle Review Chapbook* Contest and the March Hawk Press Poetry Prize.

Shane Neilson is a family physician who published his first trade book of poems in 2009. In 2010 the Porcupine's Quill published *Complete Physical* which was shortlisted for the Trillium Poetry Prize and in 2015 Neilson won the Robin Blaser Award for a long poem. In addition to several more collections of poetry, Shane Neilson has published memoirs, short fiction, biography and literary criticism, and his work has been widely anthologized in poetry, nonfiction and medical journals. In both his medical and writing practices, he focuses on mental illness, pain and disability. He acts as editor for Victoria, B.C., publisher Frog Hollow Press. Though he lives in Oakville, Ont., all of Neilson's work is rooted in rural New Brunswick.

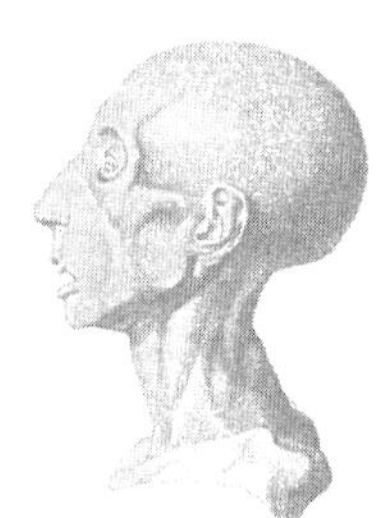